He Interrupted
My Dream
with
Destiny

TOWANDA ARMSTRONG

He Interrupted My Dream with Destiny

Trilogy Christian Publishers
A Wholly Owned Subsidiary of Trinity Broadcasting Network
2442 Michelle Drive, Tustin, CA 92780

Copyright © 2023 by Towanda Armstrong

For information, address Trilogy Christian Publishing Rights Department, 2442 Michelle Drive, Tustin, CA 92780.

Trilogy Christian Publishing/ TBN and colophon are trademarks of Trinity Broadcasting Network.

For information about special discounts for bulk purchases, please contact Trilogy Christian Publishing.

Trilogy Disclaimer: The views and content expressed in this book are those of the author and may not necessarily reflect the views and doctrine of Trilogy Christian Publishing or the Trinity Broadcasting Network.

Manufactured in the United States of America
10 9 8 7 6 5 4 3 2 1

Library of Congress Cataloging-in-Publication Data is available.

ISBN: 979-8-88738-691-1
E-ISBN: 979-8-88738-692-8

DEDICATION

To my mother and father,
Reverend Ernest V. Freeman and Lola Freeman.
Thank you for the foundation you laid for me
and the posterity you left in the earth.

TABLE OF CONTENTS

Dedication 3
Chapter 1: Preacher's Kid 7
Chapter 2: Life as a Young Mother 15
Chapter 3: There Were Detours 23
Chapter 4: When Destiny Takes Me Out of My
                 Comfort Zone. 29
Chapter 5: The Shacking Season 35
Chapter 6: Then Came Marriage... 41
Chapter 7: Starting Off on the Wrong Foot 45
Chapter 8: The Honeymoon Is OVER: One Year Later . . 53
Chapter 9: "Still a G Thang" 57
Chapter 10: My Exodus 65

CHAPTER 1

Preacher's Kid

Growing up a preacher's kid meant that there were expectations of me from my parents, from my church, and from my community. The direction my life took however, did not reflect those "standards" and I delved into a world outside of the one I grew up in, one I had no knowledge of nor ever saw any examples of from my own family, and one I never expected to be involved in. Nevertheless, I chose to embrace each season and watch as God cross pollinated His Will and plans for my life with my experiences, even when I had stepped outside of that. He has still worked it all together to reveal the jewels that were hidden within me. Not every story has ideal beginnings, but mines is certainly one of trials, triumph, growth, and FAITH!

My journey began at the age of nine when I would play church with my sister, cousins, and friends. We know kids normally play cooking, house, outside riding bikes and playing ball, but who knew that a group of children would choose to mimic ministry in their play time? Well, part of it was the fact that church was a top priority in my home growing up. Every Sunday, church attendance was mandatory of course because my daddy was a preacher. No matter what else was going on around us, like clockwork we knew we were going to hear "GET UP AND GET READY FOR CHURCH!" and we'd had better do just that.

I gained a lot through the church in my youth, to the point that I can recall a Sunday where I was playing with my friends and one of my father's deacons called me over to him to ask me questions concerning the Bible. It took me by surprise because I was still a child, and here was this grown man asking *me*, a young preteen at the time, about The Word of God.

As I progressed through my childhood, high school is when I began to see another side of the world in a way I had not seen it before then. I was introduced to another option, another way to live, and if I had to be honest, my curious and sprouting mind was excited about that. I was already known as the black sheep of the family, and being the youngest, I felt like there was nothing I did that was ever good enough for the standard set before me by my family and the church. I was a preacher's kid, but I didn't conduct myself the way everyone says we should. At this point, I looked more to be validated in the ways I saw I could be in the world, in the company of people that appreciated and seemed to accept me the way I was.

Sometime later, I met my high school sweetheart, "Jay," whom I found myself drawn to. He was a young man that had studied the Nation of Islam and was also a part of a gang. After a while, I found myself a part of that same lifestyle and it felt good to finally be included in something where people listened when I spoke and accepted the version of "me" I was evolving into. It may sound crazy, but I saw more unity in the streets as a thug than I saw in the church! I was head over heels for Jay, and he could do no wrong in my eyes. He was my "tall, dark, and handsome" standing 6'5, chocolate skin and I thought he was the best thing going! He was an all-star basketball athlete too, so you couldn't tell this girl she wasn't winning her heart's desires.

Everything seemed to be going smoothly until I began to get questions at home about when the last time was that I'd had my menstrual cycle. You never know how closely your parents may be paying attention to you, what you do and how you move on a regular basis. It had been several months before I realized she had been watching the trash cans and noticing that there were no sanitary napkins in them. Then one day she just came up to me and said, "Let's go, we're going to the doctors!"

I was shocked when she said it but also terrified because I knew I had been sexually active. I was so nervous I didn't want to take the pregnancy test when we got there.

I took a deep breath in anticipation, and the doctor looked at me and asked, "How old are you?"

I told him I was FIFTEEN YEARS OLD.

He turned to my mother, laid his hand on her shoulder, and said, "She's going to need you more now than ever. Your daughter is four months pregnant."

FOUR MONTHS PREGNANT?! Immediately tears began to flow down my face, and I felt embarrassed and ashamed. Here I am, a preacher's kid, fifteen years old, and pregnant. My biggest fear of course was what my father would say, being the pastor of the church and knowing that the congregation would have much to say about him having a pregnant daughter. I just knew I would never be looked at the same again by the church folks.

I remember having to face my dad like it was yesterday. He called me into the room and said he knew that I was pregnant. He asked me what I was planning to do with the baby and heavy with the guilt and shame I just yelled, "I don't know!" My father's response to my surprise was that I would be the mother God called me to be. All I could do was slowly lift my head in disbelief that he didn't seem to be upset the way I expected him to be. He then reminded me of the story of Mary and how young she was when she was pregnant with Jesus and explained to me that we had no control over what God intended from the foundations of the earth. He told me that what anyone else had to say about me didn't matter but that my only concern was what God was doing in my life and for me to focus on that from then, forward. This reassurance from my father made me feel better about the mountainous journey I had before me but, there was still having to tell Jay that in just five more months, he'd be a father. When I told him, he looked at me as if there was no way he could be involved, and a few days had passed before he came to and said it was time to tell his parents. Much like with my father, telling them went over smoother than what I'd anticipated, and we had their support 100%! I believe it's because they knew my background and that I was mostly a "good girl" who had made a poor choice but that I could take on the task of being a mother and that I didn't have ill ulterior motives behind it with Jay.

You know that feeling when you have a papercut after you realize it's there? Beforehand you didn't even notice it but as soon as you spot it, it stings, and you can feel its presence. That's how it was with pregnancy after finding out and telling our families. Up to that point I hadn't felt pregnant, no morning sickness or anything but the moment I found out the reality of being pregnant came to life. At this point, every day I was faced with morning sickness, body aches and probably to some degree phantom pains I assumed were associated with my pregnancy. I was just a sophomore in high school, and it had really become a task operating as a young teen from getting up in the morning to going to school, but I knew I had to press my way through. The next couple of weeks became unbearable because by this time I had made it into my sixth month and I began to feel pain in my lower abdomen that did not seem normal.

On February 14, 1990, there was a snowstorm in Chicago like no other and that day, the pain got worse. My mother ended up taking me to University of Chicago hospital where they specialized in medical matters with teen mothers. After the doctors ran tests, they discovered I had a bladder and kidney infection. They told me that I was in preterm labor and that the infection would get worse if they tried to slow it down and I stayed pregnant. At 11:58 PM Valentine's night I gave birth to a 2 lb. 1 oz. baby girl that only had a 50% chance of living. The doctor stated that all her organs were fully developed, she was just under weight, and they would have to keep her in the NICU where she would be intubated until she was able to breathe on her own and gain weight.

At this point I really didn't understand what God was trying to show me, but I was so grateful that every day I walked into the nursery I saw my baby fighting for her life. I truly believe this was the place where I began to establish a personal relationship with God, because I knew that no one could save my child except Him. As time went on, she began to breathe on her own and in a month's time she had gained about a pound and a half, which because she was premature, was extremely good according to the doctor. There was a day my mother and I walked into the nursery and my baby was no longer in the spot they kept her in during our stay there. We both began to panic! The nurse saw us and yelled across the room to calm us down telling us that she had made so much progress that she no longer needed the tubes or to be as closely monitored so she no longer needed to be in intensive care. Later in the day, the doctor came in to speak with us to let us know that she was just underweight, and we could take her home when she was four pounds. God had shown himself to me in this process in so many ways thus far, so I begin to pray more than ever asking Him for a miracle. If I had any doubt in my mind about His power before, it all vanished on Easter Sunday when the doctors released her to finally come home. She only had to have a heart monitor that would remind her to breathe because she was still so little, her body would forget to allow her to take a breath and the monitor would alert me when to shake her a little to start breathing again. Giving birth on Valentine's Day night and being able to bring her home after two months on Easter Sunday, I can honestly say l saw the true power of resurrection at a very young age.

REFLECTION

Being a teenager is full of ups and downs all by itself! Trying to navigate life, hormones, feelings, we know especially now as adults, can be quite overwhelming. Now add being a preacher's kid, a gang member, and a teen mother which each also come with their own pressures and challenges, but that was my

LIFE. Any one of these labels is a lot on its own, but to live through the combination of all four of them, you would have to know that the Hand of God is on your life!

So, today, I say to anyone that has had to or currently must face any kinds of situations like these, to be encouraged and begin to build a relationship with God. It can start as simple as a prayer for Him to show himself to you wherever you are right now and I promise you, you pray that enough and He will if He's not already. It's just us who has to have our eyes opened to what He is doing. Also know that if you have it, a support system is vital. It was those people who stepped outside of what they expected me to be or how they viewed me, that helped me stand and make it through those troubling times knowing that God is in control! If he bought you to it, he's God enough to bring you through it!

CHAPTER 2

Life as a Young Mother

In the 90s I remember there being a song called "Babies Having Babies" and I had listened to it all the time never really understanding what they were saying. Now that I had become a mother at such a young age, I understood it very well having to mother this baby around the clock. I had always been good with and enjoyed watching other people's kids, but this was totally different becoming a mother with no actual mothering experience.

My mom was there to help me figure it all out and helped me through the process every day. She would keep my daughter while I went to school and when I worked a part time job once I turned sixteen. I felt the responsibility to make sure I could afford the things she needed such as diapers, wipes, formula, clothes, etc. I was truly blessed to have my mother through all that by my side to help me grow and learn to be the mother my baby girl needed. Some days it didn't even feel like I had a child because she was with my mother so often.

I got comfortable in that, so much that I was able to hang out and get pregnant again at the age of seventeen. I could not believe I was about to go through the same thing again but the difference between the first time and this time was that my mom said that I was going to have to take full responsibility for both of my children. She was helping so much with my daughter, but when I tell you reality hit me so hard this second time around!

I still had a lot to be grateful for. My body had healed completely from my first pregnancy, and I was able to go full-term with my second. Jay was also able to be there this time as he was not the first time. I gave birth to a baby boy and his father seemed to gravitate to him instantly. I felt like it was the fact that he was a male child and men seem to favor boys over girls, but I tried not to take it personal. It was a challenge though because as a mother, I did not feel like I had an option on which gender to favor over the other and I could notice the difference in how he showed up as a father.

Now I had two children, and anybody who ever said having two is about the same as caring for one, lied! I learned the hard way that every child is very different. My daughter was quiet when she was a baby, she barely cried except when she was hungry and sleepy. My son on the other hand? It seemed like he cried nonstop the entire first year of his life! It got so bad I dropped out of school because he would cry all night and I couldn't sleep so I couldn't focus on my work at school or at home. I had just started beauty school too so I had convinced myself that I would be okay because I had no desire to do anything else in that time of my life. I pressed my way through hair school, and I just knew that was going to be enough for me since I was so good at it already and it was my side hustle.

For a while, things were going smoothly with me managing being a teen mother of two, dropped out of high school but doing well with hair, and their father was helping a lot too. That is, until one day he called me telling me his father put him out and he needed a place to live. What was I to do now that one of the things that contributed to the smooth operation of my life began to go wrong? I thought I was in love, so I did what made the most sense at the time and ended up moving out of my parent's home and into a place with him and we "played house."

That cliché that says, "you really don't know a person until you live with them," is still one of the truest things I've heard to date. I thought I knew everything about him but boy was I in for a rude awakening. I thought that I had been the only girl in his life, but as time moved on, not only did I start to find out about other females, but I learned he had a drug addiction to something we used to call wiki sticks on the streets. These were Moore cigarettes dipped in PCP, which if you're not familiar with what *that* is, it's embalming fluid. While he is the one who introduced me to marijuana, I'm glad I never joined him in partaking in this drug. It had its effects on him and watching his decline made me swear I'd never go near it myself. As if that wasn't bad enough, he was also snorting powder!

During this time, I never knew that aside from the physical ways I was in danger, I was also extremely vulnerable to the demonic realm through the experiences I had with him because of what he and I were doing. I knew all this behavior was strange and it got so bad that there were times he'd try to do crazy things to himself. There were plenty of times I'd cry myself to sleep because it was all so devastating. As I grew older, I would research the types of drugs he was doing, and their side effects, and it chilled me to my bones learning that he could've been driven to do something terrible to me or our children as well.

    I could no longer live with him because although he was not abusive toward us directly, I knew that it was not an environment that was healthy or safe. I literally feared for both mine and my children's lives. All throughout this period, I never stopped attending my father's church, so I decided to swallow my pride, as great as it was, and ask my parents to move back in with them. I was relieved that they allowed me to come back home. It wasn't until later that when I asked my children's father what the reason was that his father kicked him out that he finally told me it was because of his addiction and that he had been fighting with him. He ended up leaving to stay with a relative in the projects of Chicago and his battle with the addiction grew stronger. He helped less and less with the kids and ultimately his presence was almost nonexistent in their lives. It was hard for me to understand him at all because knowing he was taking these drugs was one thing but who he was while on the drug was a different reality. One thing I've learned for sure over the years is that no matter who it is or what the addiction, these people deal with a mental battle and eventually display signs of those battles through some form of mental illness or another, whether bought on by the drug or revealed because of it. Most times, people who are battling addiction don't realize that they are battling with demons tied to the things they wind up involved in from the side effects and the state their bodies are in during its use. Jay was my first true encounter that I've always been able to look back on as an example as I've studied these things later in life.

Motherhood at seventeen years old still ended up being a lot smoother than it should've been because my mother was there to pick up a lot of the slack. So, I would like to take moment to truly thank my mother for believing in me and seeing me for who God said I was going to be rather than who I showed up as at that time. Even after my second child, I understand her in her stance that she helped me with my first and was willing to support me but that my actions seemed to be me taking her kindness and support for granted. She told me, "I'm going to have to let you totally experience parenting on your own this time!" and sure enough, real life hit me like a ton of bricks. My mom stopped baby-sitting for me so everywhere I went I had my two babies with me, even catching the city bus in the winter. She was always there in the background while I learned how to truly parent, especially whenever both babies would get sick at the same time! I can't thank her enough for not only helping me bear the load, but for also not enabling me and allowing me the chance to learn and grow into who I was meant to be as a woman and a mother.

Now I began to reflect on what I was doing and where I was going and what I would be doing with myself. The father of my children began to get himself cleaned up and back on track and enlisted in the Navy. I was proud of him because I saw how dedicated he was doing something for himself, but it made me want to look in the mirror at myself. I felt moved to stand up for myself and start making some big decisions that would turn my life in a different direction, because if I didn't, I was surely headed for destruction. Of course, though, when he left for the Navy, I was left alone to raise my children. My father had always told me to never let anyone think that they were my only option and that's what it felt like once he left. It took me just a few months to "pull up my bootstraps" as they say, stand on my own two feet, and be the woman and mother I needed to be for myself, and for my children.

REFLECTION

Teen parenting was never an easy plight, and to become a teen mother of two was a lot. As a teen, I had already had things I needed to confront from my childhood that weighed on me but who would have time to think about that amid being a child myself and having children! To every young person who may be living a life where this could be a real possibility, take a step back, pause, and find yourself first! You're still developing and figuring out who you are, as well as learning how to navigate that person through the world around you. You won't be able to do that with children, let alone having a sexual relationship with someone who is in the same boat. Understanding before you start having sex that it comes at a high cost that you will eventually have to pay is key. Children and diseases are not the only things you risk ending up with, but soul ties are a real thing too.

Society downplays it as you becoming hyper-attached to the first person you sleep with but it's so much deeper than that. Your spirit intertwines with the people you come into both physical and emotional contact with intimately as well as the people that either of you have been with before that. Sex was intended by God to be a gift, but when we explore it outside of those bounds, it is used by the enemy to open all kinds of doors to us. We wonder why we become emotional, extreme in our display of emotions, why we feel like we can't live without a person, and it all has spiritual ties to it. I'm grateful for the things that have happened in my life up to this point; however, if I knew the spiritual implications my actions would have and the spiritual warfare I could have avoided, things would be different. Having sex out of the places within me that I really needed to let finish growing and give to God to mold the way He wanted left me carrying extra baggage with me literally and figuratively.

I can say to anyone that is battling with being accepted, let me take the time to introduce Jesus Christ to you today, He will never leave you or forsake you! Man cannot do anything for us to the capacity and in the way that Jesus can. When we seek Him rather than acceptance from people, we save ourselves a lot of the kinds of trouble you will continue to read about in the next chapters.

CHAPTER 3

There Were Detours

Just days after I turned eighteen, while I was pumping gas at a station down the street from my parent's house, an older man approached me and asked if he could pump my gas and be my man. At first, I was tickled because I knew he had to be about ten years older than me but I was still in a place of insecurity and vulnerability. He pumped my gas, and we exchanged numbers and of course, you guessed it, we started dating and became sexually involved rather quickly. He ended up being thirteen years older than me and at the time, my friends were telling me that having an older man was where it was at! He was paying my bills and giving me money even though we did not live together, and he was also caring for his grandmother who wasn't able to drive anymore. I was in need of a car, and she knew we were together, so she ended up giving me the car she was no longer able to drive. His family and I became close, and they adored me, and I fell in love with them as well.

After six months of dating, he asked me to marry him and I think at the time I was more flattered that an older man was interested in me, a younger woman with two children, and he was already providing for all three of us. I said 'yes' because it felt like something I was supposed to do knowing how much he had already done for me and the kids and how much he was willing to do for children who were not his own. I had expected that to be the trend of our lives together forever if it went that far. He called all his family and my parents together and made the announcement that he wanted to marry me, and he proposed that night with a ring. His family was so excited that they began to plan for the wedding right away and it was to take place about five and a half months from then. I knew that I cared a lot about him, and I'd appreciated the man he showed himself to be but something inside me knew that this was not really the man I was supposed to marry.

 I say this as respectfully as I know how, but there is a point in our lives that people providing for us may make us feel obligated to give them something in return, even if it is our hand in marriage. I kept trying to convince myself that I could get used to the idea of being with him and that I could love him the way he needed, the way he saw love that moved him enough to ask me to marry him. The closer the date of the wedding came, the more nervous I became. His family quickly sent out invitations, and he had purchased a dress and ordered tuxedos for himself and the men in the wedding. His brother, who was a well-known drug dealer, had offered to pay for the wedding completely so the plans began to become more and more elaborate, and our budget grew to be $25,000! So now, we were one month away from what was supposed to be one of the most exciting and anticipated days of my life that I looked forward to and that is not how I felt.

 I was sick on the inside the closer we got and exactly two weeks before the wedding, I went to my parents and told them that I didn't want to go through with the marriage. They asked me why and I just flat out told them that I did not love him the way he loved me. I did not love him enough to commit my life to him forever. When I told him, he was devastated and of course asked why I let his brother spend all the money he did, and his family put in all the effort to continue planning the wedding if I knew I didn't want to go through it. I tried to tell him that in the moment that he proposed it was on the spot and that all the excitement from his family for him was a lot. Then his family just took off planning and I didn't know how to say I didn't really want to go forth with the proposal. He was so angry with me, and I couldn't blame him, but I knew if I went forward with everything, I would be doing myself a disservice in settling for something I knew I didn't want past where it was. I also knew I would not be able to love him the way he wanted to be or the way he deserved.

While we were together, he had started regularly attending my father's church with me. There was a girl there who I'd grown up with who always talked about wishing she could have a man like him and there were many times I picked up on the jealously she didn't hesitate to display while we were together. I'm sure he was upset enough to direct the next actions towards me out of revenge, but it wasn't long before I began to see them together. Initially, I was more upset with her because we'd known each other since we were little kids. There was no regard for any kind of woman's code or simple respect considering she was someone I grew up with now dating the man I was just engaged to regardless of how or why we ended. I learned that his feelings for her were rooted in his hurt and anger from me calling off the wedding. Either way, I had nothing negative to say because I knew where my heart was and that I made what decision was best. I had always reverenced the sacredness of marriage, and I felt I would've regretted going through with it. Interestingly to say, when time passed and he saw that I was not reacting to his relationship with the girl, he broke up with her.

REFLECTION

Making life decisions from unhealthy places can drive us to unwanted people, places, and things! I learned I needed to be careful what I asked for because I got it, and it was not really what I wanted! I knew I wanted a better relationship than what I had and a stand-up guy who did what I thought a real man was supposed to do. Some things happen in our lives because God ordained it and other things happen because we wanted it so bad, that God will allow us to get it. We ultimately learn that what we want and what God wants isn't always the same thing and that what we want isn't always what is best for us even when we think it is! He'll let us get a glimpse of what we want, especially when we continue to put our preferences before His plans and become so distracted that we're operating solely out of our own will. My words of wisdom here are to pray for it, be specific, then wait until God gives you direction. He does not author in confusion and His timing is perfect timing. He will give you a clear enough answer that you will keep seeking His face either for the next step or for confirmation in the things HE directs you to and through. I'm grateful here for God's grace and mercy because I now know that the "something" that was telling me not to go forward was Him stirring in my spirit to make the decision that ended up being right for me. We can avoid some seasons and the length we must spend in them if we would just seek what God's path is for us through prayer instead of settling for the self-willed extended detours of our own desires.

CHAPTER 4

When Destiny Takes Me Out of My Comfort Zone

When I was nineteen, I got my first apartment by myself. It felt so good to make such an adult decision, paying my own bills and taking care of my two small children by myself and not having to answer to anybody for anything! Things were going so well with me doing hair, especially after graduating cosmetology school, considering I didn't have a high school diploma. That kept me on my toes, so I always made sure I had work to do with what I loved and thought I would be doing for the rest of my life. I thought I'd be a platform stylist traveling the world to display my craft teaching, modeling my skills in hair shows and showcases, and everything in my life at that time lined up for me to be able to accomplish that goal. I was doing hair out of my home and was making at least $1,500 a week at one point. This went on for about a year and everything genuinely was going so well again. My life was starting to make sense and I was beginning to see the dreams I had years prior, slowly but surely come to pass.

Up to now, my relationship with God had grown in numerous ways and I still wanted to seek Him further and grow more in Him. Honestly it felt good enough to be where I was in my single season and thriving in my life. Then, I was driving down the street one day and I heard the Holy Spirit say, "The next man that comes onto you will not only be your husband, but he will be your assignment!" IT BLEW MY MIND! Right after that, it made me nervous because I wasn't even looking to be married, I was doing good all by myself! Months would go by, and I'd receive confirmation because every man that I actually thought was attractive and wanted to approach me never would and after a while I just said forget it! I was confused because I know God said it was going to happen, but it was like suddenly I wasn't getting the attention I thought I'd be getting since He said it. Three or four more months went by, and I had just about forgotten what the Lord had spoken to me. Later, I was riding around with my favorite cousin that I hung out with often and I got a page on my beeper. We stopped at 71st and Ashland at a Chicago gas station so that I could use the pay phone to call the guy who paged me.

    I don't know what it is about gas stations at this point but if you recall, that seems to be a common place thus far in my life for the most interesting of things to happen! While I was on the phone, I heard someone say from behind me, "instead of talking to that guy, why don't you give me a call?!" I turned around and saw this guy bent down putting air in his tires. I got off the phone and walked over to see what he was about. As he approached, I noticed he had on all kinds of jewelry, and he had finger waves in his hair. Of course, being a hairdresser, I asked, "who did your hair?!" He told me who did it, asked my name and I told him my name was Towanda and his name was Bradley. He asked me if he could take me out and I responded flirtatiously but semi curiously "if your woman doesn't mind!" That prompted him to tell me how the only woman in his life was his grandmother and that he had recently lost his mother in a car accident. Right away my heart softened up and was filled with compassion for him and after a little more conversation I told him I would go out with him. I wasn't attracted to him as much as other guys I'd usually date but what was the harm in giving him the time to take me out, right?

That next evening, we went to a club together and he wined and dined me, which I enjoyed. As the night ended though, I noticed he looked like he wasn't feeling well. He said as much, so I invited him to my apartment for soup, medicine, and relax to feel better and by the time we made it there, he was drenched in sweat and had a fever. I let him stay in my bed and I slept in my daughter's bed that night. As I was laying in her bed that next morning, I heard the Lord say, "THIS is your husband and your assignment..." I WAS DISAPPOINTED! I thought to myself, *God this can't be! I'm not even attracted to this man!* Heck, he had four flat tires when I met him, which I later learned was from two different women slashing them! I could barely process what I'd heard from God before Bradley called out my name from the next room like something was wrong, so I ran to see what was going on. He said he'd felt better, and his fever broke and was thanking me for taking care of him the way I did. He told me I reminded him of his mother and that it moved him, and he knew from that, that he wanted me to be his wife! Right then it hit me like a flash of movie scenes where I remembered what God spoke to me initially a few months prior and then again just moments before. What I wanted to say was, "No, I don't want to be married!" but it was like my mouth wouldn't move and I knew it was God not allowing me to speak. He kept going on and on and finally said that I needed to come and meet his grandmother so that we could get her approval. I was just speechless. Just like that it had all happened according to what God spoke to me and I didn't know what else to do other than to move forward in it.

We went to his grandmother's house, and she was outside sitting on the porch. As soon as she saw me, she got up, mumbled something under her breath, went in the house, and slammed the door! Bradley said she was just upset he didn't come home the night before and didn't call her to let her know he was okay. In my mind, I kept telling myself, *This can't be God!* He went in the house after her and told her he'd be moving out and she started to fuss at him, yelling, "You don't know nothing about this girl! You are crazy!" As I sat there listening to the conversation, my stomach turned, and I went inside myself asking God if He was sure this man was it! No response… The longer I sat listening, I learned he'd been with a lot of women by the things his grandmother was yelling at him. I begin praying asking God, "what have I gotten myself into!" All I kept hearing was husband and assignment.

REFLECTION

There will be times when life takes an unfamiliar turn and we do not understand where we're headed or why we're headed in those directions. In these times, the best thing for us to do is ask God to order our steps and allow Him to show us what to do and where to go, even when it doesn't look the way we want it to or thought it would. That's how I would describe this season. I wasn't quite sure why God had me marrying this man but once I heard that he was my assignment, I knew there had to be something bigger going on. Even when I wanted to rebel, in that moment God disabled my ability to do so! That looks different for everybody. You ever have your mind set on one plan and something happens that stops that plan from going according to the way you saw it playing out? Flat tire on the way to someone's house? A family emergency coming up when you already had plans that you ended up having to cancel?

Sometimes, the least likely route is the way God has for us to go to either teach us something or grow us in some way. The best reaction to have once He gives you confirmation is to say, "Lord not my will but your will be done in my life!" It will save you a lot of heart ache and headache long term. Again, I warn, be careful what you attach to throughout your life and what you allow to attach to you. All God wants to do is lead and guide you into the great things HE has for you but sometimes we're too busy operating in our own will and making choices out of places void of God, rather than allowing Him to be the foundation on which we build our lives. One way or another, He will direct things to happen to get your undivided attention and essentially you are still able to hear His voice and receive direction from Him that will align you to where you are supposed to be.

CHAPTER 5

The Shacking Season

Just when I thought I had a grip on life, I found myself in an unfamiliar and uncomfortable place. In a matter of three days, I now had a whole family; me, my two children, and a man I didn't even really know! A few months had passed before I told Bradley what God had shown me about the next man that came into my life and how I'd be married to him and how he was my assignment. Neither of us fully grasped what that meant, but we saw eye to eye on being together and I only hoped it was a good sign for the things to come. The kids took to him quickly and I was truly grateful for that. He and I got along well, and things seemed like they weren't so bad,

I became more and more excited as time went by. It felt good to have help with the children and to feel like an actual family. We were still going out with each other to the club and on dates and about six months into the relationship I remember one night where Bradley said, "Babe, let's go to my old spot tonight." Of course, I agreed because I had such a positive outlook on our relationship thus far that I saw it as just a chance to see where he used to hang out before he and I got together. Little did I know that I'd learn more about him alright, but not in the way a woman wants to know about the man God has assigned to her in marriage.

We were dancing together in the club and a pregnant woman walked by me and bumped into me. I didn't pay attention at first, I just kept on dancing, that is, until she came back by and did it again. I turned that time and told her to watch where she was going and she responded, "I'll do it again!" Right then, Bradley grabbed me and told me it was time to go. I was confused because he didn't say anything to her but once we got to the car he turned and went back into the club, and immediately I thought to myself, *I smell a rat!* When he came back, I asked him who she was and he told me flat out that it was a girl he'd messed with before we got together and he had gotten her pregnant. I was so ANGRY! How could he not think it was appropriate to mention that he had a baby on the way any day now amid all the talk about wanting me to be his wife and meeting his grandmother and moving in! That seemed too big a detail to just accidentally leave out even in the short amount of time we'd known each other. He proceeded to tell me that there was nothing between the two of them and that it just happened. I couldn't help but to recall those flat tires and how when he moved in with me, his grandmother strongly disagreed with him doing so. I was so hurt, and I began to look at myself funny as if maybe I misheard God on this one. I didn't speak to him the whole ride home and when we pulled up, he told me that I wasn't going to go into the house without speaking to him.

I thought he had a lot of audacity considering the situation and the fact that it was my apartment to begin with, but I still didn't have anything to say to him. When we got to the door, as soon as I unlocked it, he pushed me out of the way and into the hallway and pulled my shirt off and yelled, "I TOLD YOU, YOU CAN'T COME HOME UNTIL YOU TALK TO ME!" Thank God I lived on a three-story flat on the third floor where no one could see me outside half naked! I was outside of my own home banging on the door begging this man to come in. He yelled through the door, "Are you ready to talk?!" and I yelled back, "YES, I'LL TALK!" I was so hurt, and I didn't have anyone I wanted to tell something like that happened and nowhere to go with how I felt but still I told God I would trust Him.

Two weeks later the girl had the baby, and he went to see them at the hospital but the girl's mother would not allow him to see either of them. He came home angry and picked a fight with me for no reason. It hurt because at the time I didn't know what was going on, I was completely in the dark. He had a drink and calmed down and although it didn't occur to me back then, this was the first time I had seen him use alcohol to desensitize himself. I began to tell myself things would get better with time and after we got married and then we wouldn't be shacking up. Maybe then we'll be doing it the right way because we'll be married the way God said we were supposed to be and then maybe he'd start to display characteristics of a man of God if we both were in better alignment. I talked to him about how I felt, and he agreed to get married. I just focused on the word I had received, "husband and assignment."

REFLECTION

There is so much to unpack here starting with the unwise decision to move in with someone before ever getting to know them or build a friendship with them before jumping into a marriage together. My case was a bit different because at the time I was following where I sensed God was leading me. Before you make major decisions in your life and in your single season, submit to the Will of God so you don't have to bear the extra burden of the consequences that come with Him having to reconstruct your path from the times you went astray. Really, you should be praying about every relationship that you enter and for spiritual discernment on the progress of that relationship. Normally, you would not meet a person, move in with them a few days later, then proceed to plan a life with them not knowing much about them, and certainly not finding out the things that I soon learned were a part of his lifestyle and who he was.

Next is God's Plan versus our own plans! If someone was in these same circumstances and didn't hear from God, they'd look exactly alike, right!? So, I'm sure you're thinking *how this could be God!* The thing about our Lord is that He operates in a way that works out best for us in the long run and sometimes that looks rough based on our lifestyle or previous decisions up to that point. It's not that God was saying, "I'm going to punish you with a terrible husband because of anything you've ever done in your life," but more like he was going to put me in a season where, even though I didn't see it at the time, I could only focus on Him. I could only focus on wherever it was I wanted to go beyond where I was at that time, because as you see I found out rather swiftly that was not where I wanted to be. I choose to see this season as a time that I was on an assignment as God called me to be in the role as a wife and God would let me know how to make it through the assignment, what its purpose was, and how this assignment was going to grow me and bring me closer to him. Ultimately, God used this as an opportunity for me to strengthen my relationship with Him.

CHAPTER 6

Then Came Marriage...

We started out planning for a wedding ceremony, but we ended up just going to the courthouse and having a small reception ceremony in his aunt's backyard. He wanted to marry me on my birthday, but it was on a Monday that year, so we had to wait until that Friday which ended up being April 12, 1996. Nervous was not even the beginning of what I felt that entire week because all I could think about was the year leading up to where we were, dealing with baby momma drama, drinking, street life, and cheating! I stood firm on the word God gave me that he was going to be my husband and that this was my assignment.

During this time, we lived in Madison, Wisconsin and all our family was back in Chicago so that's where we were going to get married. When Friday came, we rounded up the family in the conversion van we had at the time. It was only a year old and had 40,000 miles on it, so it was to my surprise, when travelling the two hours from Madison to Chicago, that one hour into the trip, a loud noise came from the front of the car and a big poof of smoke came up from the hood! Thank goodness that my dad owned a towing company at the time and sent a towing truck to our rescue.

Immediately I was thinking, *God, of all days on the day of my wedding? Is this a sign to not marry him?* Of course, I didn't get a response, maybe because I already knew what I wanted to hear Him say back to me. The van wouldn't start at all, so it had to be put on the back of the flat bed of the tow truck. There were too many of us to all fit in the tow truck and even though it was illegal to do, we put the kids in the tow truck and Bradley and I rode in the van on the back. After we got that situated, we pressed on to the courthouse and once we arrived, my husband to be started saying he didn't feel good.

By this time, I was ready to just say forget it, there was already so much that happened in that one day and I was wishing I'd just stayed in bed instead. It was hard not to challenge that this was what God was telling me to do now! We went through with the ceremony though and as soon as we got finished, he said, "I'm about to throw up!" He started to vomit everywhere and at this point, all I could do was think, *Well, I'm married to him now.*

REFLECTION

In an ideal preparation for marriage, it would be a wonderful opportunity for both soon to be spouses to have open discussions about what their thoughts and feelings are. It would've been nice to discuss any reservations or have a conversation to talk about where your minds are before saying "I do." Otherwise, already before the covenant starts, you are setting yourself up for issues in the realm of communication. Even with this being something that I felt God led me to do, it would've been better to prepare for what was ahead of us. We had some of the tools around us but neither of us used them. When entering a union with someone in general, one of the best things you can do is to seek spiritual counseling within the church you attend. If you trust the leadership of that ministry to minister to your spirit and help you with your spiritual growth, you should also be able to trust them to guide you in how to approach one of the most sacred and cherished covenants we could make with another person and before God. Proper preparation prevents poor performance in the long run, and though marriage comes with its own set of challenges, it helps going into it with eyes and hearts wide open about what to expect from both the woman and man who are going to be involved in it.

CHAPTER 7

Starting Off on the Wrong Foot

What God had just spoken to me a year prior was now a reality and here we were, day one, he'd thrown up all over the grass of the courthouse. We didn't know that the driver who was sent to tow us was going to tie cans with string on the back of the truck and write "Just Married" on the back window of the van to celebrate but it didn't feel like much of a celebration. We had planned on spending that night on the waterfront then stay in a fancy hotel in downtown Chicago but all that was out the window and we both felt some type of way about how the day went. We ended up going to my parents' house and when we arrived, we were well into it with one another. I called the same cousin I was with the night I met Bradley and he called his cousin that lived nearby as well. We went our separate ways for a few hours and agreed to meet back up at midnight. I needed to step away from the situation and process what all had happened throughout the course of that day and how much had changed within a twenty-four-hour period. About nine that night, I had it in my heart to apologize for my part in the argument and just extend empathy for how the day had gone. I tried to call him a few times, but he wasn't answering his phone. In fact, hours had gone by and around eleven p.m. I still wasn't getting a response, so the anger welled up inside me all over again. I asked my cousin to take me back to my parents' house to check for him there but he wasn't there. Midnight came and went and still no Bradley. I started to think about divorce already but as clear as day I heard God say, "DIVORCE WILL NOT BE AN OPTION!" I screamed out in frustration because I wanted to hear Him earlier when I was asking if all the unfortunate things happening that day was a sign, but now there was no mistaking hearing him in that instance. "I CAN'T DO THIS GOD!" but again, there was no response...

 I began to think about how I got here and contemplating hard again about whether I heard God correctly before I had gone forth with the marriage. Surely God didn't mean for me to spend the one night that every girl and woman dreams of, alone! The doubt constantly crept in, and I wanted so bad for God to tell me that I had misheard Him, but I never heard Him confirm the doubt.

 I didn't hear from my husband until 8:30 the next morning. He called my phone and tried to passively ask me, "How's my wife doing this morning? Are you still angry with me?" Just as casual as he could like everything that happened didn't happen and like nothing was wrong. He proceeded to tell me that he didn't answer his phone because he was just so distraught and upset that he didn't have the words. He then asked me if my brother was around and if he could speak to him. My brother gets off the phone and tells me that Bradley asked him to come pick him up from his ex-girlfriend's house. The blatant disrespect for him to not only ask my brother to come and get him but of all places from his ex-girlfriend's house! I decided to get in the car with my brother and ride with him to the house that my husband had decided to spend our wedding night at. His ex-came out on the porch when we pulled up and I hopped out of the car ENRAGED ready to fight! As soon as I was moving toward the house, I heard a voice tell me "GET BACK IN THE CAR, THIS IS ONLY A TEST!" So, I turned and got in the backseat to go back to the house.

The whole ride, I could tell he was anxious and just trying to strike up meaningless small talk to distract away from the fact that we were leaving from picking him up from his ex's house on day one of our marriage after he spent our wedding night with another woman. Reality sank in further as I stared out the window thinking that this was something I'd be seeing a lot more of throughout our marriage. I was disappointed, my feelings were hurt, and I felt so alone, but still, I was so committed to what I had heard God say and even the things he spoke since that moment, that I chose to stand firm in the process, even when I didn't understand it at all.

We ended up having to spend those next few days in Chicago because the engine was blown up in our van that broke down. I was angry each of those days we spent there but I was hearing a lot more of God now telling me not to shy away from my new life as a wife. He'd told me that I had obligations now and I couldn't neglect them no matter how this man made me feel and despite how he was treating me. It was a tough pill to swallow but still, I had to make up my mind to fully commit to the process I had ahead of me. Eventually, we returned home and already had begun to plan a reception for all our families to be there, so we chose September 28th for the date to celebrate being newly married. When that day arrived, we had a cake that had a bride and groom topper on it and at some point, with all of us in the house, we went to cut our cake and the bride and groom were no longer on the cake. Someone had stolen the bride and groom from our cake and one of my aunts thought it was the funniest thing. It was so odd to me because it wasn't like there were kids around to have stolen it or anything like that! We joked about it for some time, but I knew it had to have a deeper meaning behind it happening at all.

I mean thinking back on the things that had happened the night we went out together, on our way to get married, and right after we got married, it seemed to be just another sign of the times to come but I figured I'd just have to wait for it all to play out. On September 29th, we went on our honeymoon to the Bahamas on a four-day cruise with a two day stop in Disney. The last night that we were on the ship, there was a huge storm on the sea and the captain announced that this kind of storm had not been recorded for the last twenty-five years! They instructed everyone to go back to their rooms and lie in bed because the boat was moving so much that no one could stand safely. I laid in that bed praying to God to just be able to make it back home in one piece, and He reminded me of the story of Jonah. While God allowed circumstances to happen around him that seemed to him like all was lost, He was using each of those circumstances to bring Jonah closer to Him and align him with His Will! He began to speak to me and tell me to start looking at my life this way; to start viewing this assignment through this lens. In that moment, He was renewing my spirit to remind me also that He would be with me through it all. I was not receptive right away because my feelings and my thoughts were, "God, if life is supposed to make me feel the same way this cruise is making my stomach feel I don't know if I want to go want to go through it!" It's funny to think back on where I was then nevertheless, I PRESSED my way through.

Since I had grown up in church, I shifted and started to think back on similar stories to my situation outside of what God had just spoke to me and I remembered Paul in a boat with the sailors in a terrible storm before it shipwrecked. The storm started out so badly that when the sailors tried to take control of the ship, there was a wind that blew so fiercely that they had no choice but to let go and let the storm take the boat wherever it would. The storm took place over the course of about two weeks and all throughout its duration, they tried to do different things to relieve themselves of the turmoil it caused by tossing over supplies they needed to maintain the boat. They still wanted to control where they might end up even when they had no control over the boat. Interesting logic, don't you think? Paul then gathers the sailors together and encourages them by telling them that the previous night an angel told him that God would save their lives, but the boat would be destroyed. Even in that word from God, when they saw land was near, they tried to use the lifeboat that had trailed behind them the whole trip.

They ended up letting down too much weight trying to slow the boat to a stop and were afraid they would crash into rocks. At this point they started trying to abandon ship and Paul told the captain that the only way every life was going to be saved was if every sailor remained on the boat. The sailors cut the weighted line, and the lifeboat from the ship and let it all drift away. Paul encouraged them to nourish themselves because everyone had been so preoccupied worrying about the storm none of them ate that whole time. He reassured them of the word he got from God, that not a single hair on their head would be harmed and so they ate. They eventually saw land again that next morning and the boat began to crash, so the sailors wanted to kill every prisoner to prevent their escape once they landed, but because of wanting to spare Paul, the captain didn't let them do that. Instead, he ordered everyone to jump into the water after the wreck. Some swam, others drifted on broken wood, but they made it safely to the shore.

As for Bradley and me, we made it back safely but we both got sick because of the change in the weather from the Bahamas back to the cool of October in Madison. Even so, that story encouraged me the same way Paul encouraged those sailors. I knew God was just going to use all this to prepare me for my destiny! I had to take heart that I'd be able to learn, grow, and minister my way through this marriage!

REFLECTION

Don't let what I'm about to say make you shy away from getting closer to God, but sometimes, following God can be as painful as not following Him at all. The difference between the two is that the pain of being refined and prepared for His Will is a lot better than the pain of dealing with the consequences of not living aligned with it and sinking in sin. This is when we should all be encouraged to remember that we all have our very own crosses to bear. No matter who you are, where you are, what your age is, or what season of your life you are in, there are going to be some things that come your way to test your faith! BE ENCOURAGED! God never promised us that it would be easy, but He did promise that we'd be able to enjoy it the most when it is HE who lays the foundation, perfects our faith, and bring us into His intended becoming for who He purposed us to be!

CHAPTER 8

The Honeymoon Is OVER: One Year Later

Like I just said, the road was not easy, by any means. I can recollect many of our arguments throughout this marriage but our first and biggest fight started over Bradley not wanting me to go out to the club. He was picking a fight about it because the woman he was messing around with was going to be there that night. I wasn't hearing anything he was saying because I already knew what I was going to wear, and just spent about six hours doing my hair in this up-do finished off with rhinestones, and I was ready for the night! He persisted in telling me I wouldn't be going anywhere, that I'd be staying home taking care of the kids and his brother that he had taken custody of when his mother passed. I began to challenge him and respond by telling him I didn't know who he thought he was talking to but that he was not the boss of me. I walked away and went upstairs, and he got even more angry and started cursing me out and stormed into the kitchen. I had been working on dinner throughout the day making cabbage and corned beef and had just finished cleaning the kitchen.

I heard him still fussing and cussing as I was coming back down the stairs and as I watched him come out of the kitchen with a bucket of dirty mop water I hadn't poured out yet, he raised it up and dumped it over my head… I was devastated! I couldn't believe he would actually do something like that to me, but I began to see red.

I was so angry that I went into the kitchen myself and looked right at the corn beef and just in a split second knew I was either going to dump this scolding hot water on him or else I felt like I would kill him! I began to gain just a little bit of clarity to not land myself in jail, but my mind shifted to getting him back somewhere else. I knew what I was about to do would hurt him as much as me giving him third degree burns from the corned beef water. He loved his cars, honestly, more than he loved me, so instead of potentially doing a bid, I poured the cabbage into the corned beef, took it outside, and tossed it all over the inside of his car! The dashboard, the seats, the floor, EVERYWHERE!

Needless to say, that night ended with neither one of us going anywhere because my hair and now his car were both messed up.

REFLECTION

This could've easily played out a different way either for the worst or the best but for us it was a "tit for tat" situation that went too far. He didn't want me to find out about the other woman he had at the time, and I refused to allow him to speak to me the way he was and try to make demands of me as if I was his child that he makes decisions FOR rather than his wife with whom he makes decisions WITH. His response to that was wrong and my response back to his response was wrong and thank goodness it didn't go any further than that in extremity. Revenge is an emotional state that can cost you your life and we've all felt the need some time or another to get someone back for mistreating us or in retaliation for a wrongdoing. The danger of being in a place of revenge is some of us go through these same situations but don't make it out of them alive. He could've easily responded violently like he had the night I found out he had another woman pregnant, and I didn't want to speak to him. In the heat of the moment, we do what we feel is best and that is not always the best decision. God gives us guidance on this specifically for these reasons and more. He lets us know in His word that vengeance is His and that He will indeed repay those who have done us wrong for their wrongdoing in due time if we would only let him handle it. There are times we avenge ourselves thinking we are doing ourselves a justice and defending our own honor, but we take away from God's person when we try to take matters into our own hands. We also put ourselves at risk for the unknown and threatening, sometimes fatal reactions of someone else's instability. We may not know how or when, but it is through our faith and trust in Jesus and staying still in Him that we have the ultimate victory in letting Him handle our business.

CHAPTER 9

"Still a G Thang"

Now recall, that all the while through this time, I was still a gang member. It was not a life that I chose to relinquish simply because of marriage or my relationship with God, nor was it really an option. The Bible makes it clear in scripture in a remixed variation, that you can take a person out of the city, but you can't take the city out of the person "except they be born again with the fire of the Holy Ghost." Down inside, and even on the outside when provoked, I was still a thug! When you're in a gang, you learn through experience about territories and how when you're given a territory, you are supposed to guard it with your life and stand for it at all costs! This was a principle that carried through all the areas of my life, to include my family, my children, and my husband.

It was November 8, 1997, Bradley's birthday, and we were preparing to celebrate him at a local spot we'd gone to a few times before. When we got there, our favorite bartender was working and told him that since it was his birthday, we could both have a drink on the house. I decided to try something a little different and ordered a well-known dry gin, with lime. The drink was okay and the more I drank, the more laid back I thought I'd feel but I was getting frustrated. I noticed that as the night went on, this same girl kept making flirtatious eye contact with my husband and I was feeling dangerously territorial. I leaned over to my girlfriend who came with us and started to go off like the gangster I truly was. "I SWEAR ON EVERYTHING I LOVE IF THIS CHICK DON'T STOP LOOKIN' AT HIM, I'M GOING TO DO DAMAGE!" It wasn't until the end of the night when we were all leaving out of the club that I saw her make her way past us and squeeze in front of my husband as we were all coming out the door.

I went into an alcohol encouraged rage because up to that point I could easily just remind myself that this was my God given assignment and just another "casualty of war," but not this night. I snatched him up by his collar so fast, yanked him back into the bar, walked up behind her and snatched her by the hair, and smacked her in the face. She went flying across the table and got up quickly holding her face and when she put her hand down to say something I saw I'd left my handprint on her cheek!

She yelled "I WAS JUST PLAYING AROUND WE ARE FRIENDS!"

I replied, "HE ALREADY HAS A FRIEND, ME! YOU GOT THAT?!"

Everybody that came with us didn't know whether to egg me on because I "G Checked" her or be scared that someone had called the police because I'd made a scene. At that point, I didn't care at all because I was fed up and honestly, I might've gotten her for the old and the new things she wasn't even involved in all the way up to that moment that she was. Despite being slightly driven by the alcohol, most of my actions were just me being tired of choosing to be silent and so I chose to take matters into my own hands! That was how I told myself from that point forward I'd be dealing with things. I chose to stay the course, but I'd be handling things *my* way. After this, I began to retaliate his aggressive anger with my own violent anger. We argued all the time and most of the arguments turned into fights. My way was definitely not the best, but it was how I felt like I was letting him know I wasn't going to keep taking his mess quietly and I felt good standing up for myself!

On top of my still being a part of the gang I was in; Bradley was in the gang too and was a well-known drug dealer. At one point, over a period of a year and a half I knew he made over half a million dollars! The lifestyle we lived seemed to be good and we were what kids these days like to call "couple goals" when they see us as icons but have no idea what darkness and pain is being endured on the inside and behind the scenes. A lot of people think they want this life with the flashy jewelry, cars, houses, and clothes obtained by the street life. This kind of lifestyle where we believe we have what we think are the best things in life and we get to call ourselves "self-made" in trying to acquire them. It's not all it's cracked up to be by any means. We had moved away from the area where the gang was, so direct activity was no longer something we were too much faced with, but those mentalities stuck with us. We still represented by wearing colors and when we ran into opposite gangs there were still things we said or did that let them know "what set we repped."

Both things alone could've cost us our lives, but it didn't matter to us because it was what we both grew up in. There was one weekend where we pulled up to a gas station while we went home to Chicago for a visit, and it was within two blocks of the opposite gang. Our gang territory was only three blocks away but because we were riding with a "strap" we thought that would be enough to defend ourselves, if need be, but we underestimated that need. My husband got out to pump the gas, not knowing that some members of the gang whose territory we were in rode by and saw us. This was during a time when our hairdos were another way to identify who was in what gang and Bradly had finger waves in his hair which was a representation of our gang. Once they saw that, I'm assuming that's what triggered them to pull up and hop out of the car with guns. There were a few people in the car with us too so when they did this, he did not pull out the gun he was carrying, but instead, jumped back into the car and sped off. I was so grateful to escape that situation with our lives, but I also started to think that maybe it was time to think about leaving the gang life behind.

The next situation that showed me was similar. We liked our cars to be flashy to show everybody "what we were working with." We had a short body Cadillac with gold rims, gold nose, and a gold face so it was easily identifiable because of the specific finishes. My parents had a situation where their car broke down, so we lent them this Cadillac. My dad was excited because he used to say, "every preacher should drive a Caddy!" He went out to drive it to church one Sunday morning and two young guys walked up to him and asked where he got the car from. He told them he was borrowing it from his son-in-law and they asked him what he thought his son-in-law would do if he didn't get the car back. Thank God the police happened to be circling the block and stopped because they said they saw concern and worry in my dad's face. God provided a way out that day, not just for Dad, but for me and Bradley too. My dad called us right after and said, "Come and get this car NOW and I mean right now! I don't want no parts of it! I almost lost my life today!"

Finally, there was an incident that really showed me I was being warned. We had a two-seater droptop mustang with gold rims, very nice. We were driving on I-90 doing about 85 miles an hour. Suddenly, the back tire on the driver side popped right off the car and passed us on the highway in the grass! We were going so fast that we had no choice but to then slam on the brakes WHILE we slid on the hub accessory of the missing wheel! Right then and there I said, "OKAY GOD, YOU HAVE MY UNDIVIDED ATTENTION!"

As time continued, I was still involved but slowly putting down those things that I was used to doing with drug dealing and gang way of living. I was doing very well as a stylist and owned my first salon, The Untouchable 2, with myself and a friend of mine. We were popular and in high demand because Madison was a small college town, and we were good at what we did to where I could easily make $1,400-$2000 a day! Unfortunately, just 'as well-known we were in the streets, we had gained popularity with the law too as involved as we had been over the years. Even when I began to part from the street life, there were still people who seemed to not like that we were doing better and running in the streets less. I had to keep a stash of bail money laid to the side because Brad ending up in jail became a norm. There were reports of him selling drugs during a time that he in fact was not.

The issue was that we hadn't let it all go completely and could still be placed in that lifestyle as a result. Then, the next big fight we had ended with me needing to go to the hospital and get stitches over my left eye when my husband threw a ceramic vase at my face. The doctors told me that if the vase had struck me just a half a centimeter lower, it would've cost me my eye, so eight stitches seemed like a good alternative to be able to keep my eyesight. In hindsight, neither one of those should've been an option considering it happened at the hands of the man who claimed to love me and to this day you can still see that scar over my left eye. Between the street trouble, cheating and the fighting, we decided that it was too much and moved away from Madison.

REFLECTION

What amazes me about God is that even when we are living outside His will, He still loves us enough to give us a glimpse of the glory that He wants to reveal in our lives. While I truly believed, trusted, and loved God in and out of every season, I still dealt with things that were a part of what should've been an old life to me. I didn't let go of the gang or the lifestyle, mindsets, or practices attached to it and operating that way, I was serving two masters. This is a prime example of being lukewarm, where I trusted God enough to hear from Him and receive blessings from Him but not enough to let go of one of the things that I became a part of from a voided place in my life. These were things I clung to since I was a teenager needing that kind of connection and validation. When we are in a place where we don't realize it or where we are ignoring the more subtle ways God tries to alert us of this duplicity, the warnings become greater. I thank God now for being so patient and gracious to call me all the way out of the ways of the world I was still living in. Trials and tribulations in general are an inevitable part of all our lives. It is through both that our relationship with God can deepen and grow stronger. Over every mountain He has brought me and even every valley I ended up in because of my own doing, it was these experiences that enabled me to say today what it says in Psalms 34! I WILL bless the Lord AT ALL TIMES and His praises shall CONTINUALLY be in my mouth!

CHAPTER 10

My Exodus

We had moved to Milton, Wisconsin which was only about forty minutes outside of Madison but still the change of scenery we figured we needed. I always wanted to have a house on the side of a highway, and I'd finally gotten it! I had my "dream house" on nine acres of land and on the outside, it seemed like I had everything a wife could ever want. The truth is, everything that glitters isn't gold, and I was in a dark place where I felt broken and depressed. There were things missing from our marriage, but the biggest component we lacked was having a mutual and united relationship together that included God. It never mattered how much stuff we had accumulated, I felt like I was dying inside, and I couldn't even bring myself to pray about it. I mean, what would I say to God that He didn't already know when He told me this was my assignment? What good would praying about this do now? Six months had gone by, and I was constantly in this emotional state.

I remember one day sitting outside on our tire swing when no one else was home, the kids were in school, my husband was at work, and I just sat there staring up at the sky. It was so bright and blue and full of clouds, and I sat gazing into it drifting away from everything around me and the things happening in my mind. Suddenly, the clouds began to separate like there was a strong wind blowing but there wasn't, and once they parted, I heard a voice speaking to me! It said, "Leave everything and go to Kentucky…" It scared me so bad I fell backwards out of the swing and my feet got stuck in the tire but all I could do was stare at the sky wondering if I'd really heard what I just heard! Again, that same voice repeated, "Leave everything and go to Kentucky…" I knew then that it was God speaking to me in a way He had never spoken to me before and I began to sob uncontrollably. The first thing my mind went to was how I had accomplished so much to get to where I was at in this stage of my life. Then it was how I would explain to my husband that God said to leave everything and just go! Before I could move on to my next worry in my flood of concern, a peace like I'd never felt before washed over me and in my spirit. I felt a shift to where my answer to the questions I had and to what God just said were "Yes, Lord." My spirit was willing, but my flesh was at war with the thoughts that kept coming in. We had just gotten our house set up the way we both wanted it to be, the salon was doing very well, but we can't even get along on a consistent basis, how do I know he would even hear me out or accept this notion?

Later that evening when he got home, I told him what happened and what I knew I heard God say. His response to me was ultimately a harsh no. "I'm not moving to no Kentucky! I'll move back to Chicago before I would ever live in Kentucky!" I didn't poke at the matter beyond that and immediately, I started to pack up the house. I called my parents and shared with them what God had told me and they told me, much like my father responded to my being pregnant when I was fifteen, that my only concern, no matter what, was to make sure I was following the instruction and Will of God. Their encouragement only pushed me further into my decision to obey so being in right standing with the Master was my main priority. My husband was very clear on his decision to not move to Kentucky, and he kept stating that he was not going to change his mind. He had insulted me and called me stupid and crazy because it could not have been God to tell me to do something so "foolish" when we had just gotten established in Milton and what we had built.

I didn't budge, my mind was so made up, I called my only sister who lived in Kentucky at this time and told her that I was moving there and that I was coming for a visit that weekend to search for an apartment. Sure enough, I rented a car and made my way down south. I must've been on my apartment hunt for what seemed like five minutes before I found a place, found favor with the landlord, and had signed a lease to rent for no money down. As soon as I secured that I was able to set up utilities and a phone and by the time I left to return home, it was all set up for me to move in. This let me know that it had to be nothing but the will of God for everything to fall into place so easily and quickly. Since my husband was in such opposition to the move, I did not tell him how smoothly things went over the weekend and how successful the trip was because I didn't want to get into a fight. I did let him know that I was moving for sure and that there was nothing he could do about it. The rest of the day was still spoiled because he did not like how sure I was about following the instruction I'd received from the Lord whether he agreed or not.

He was going off fussing and cussing me out saying that the marriage was over and not to come looking for him because he would not be there if I came back. He threatened to leave me first and move to Chicago and take all our things with him. I tried to speak reason with him and tell him that I wasn't being spiteful or trying to leave him but that I was only trying to be obedient and follow what I felt in my spirit and heard with my own ears God was telling me to do for us. His response was to go and rent a moving truck of his own and pack up everything he could squeeze into it. I told him it didn't matter and that the only thing I really wanted was the fish tank that we had because it was a beautiful aquarium and I had already started to picture it in the new apartment I rented. I could already begin to visualize myself in the next destination God was calling me to and the only thing I even cared about coming other than my children, was my aquarium! At the end of all the packing and fussing, we just agreed to go to my parent's home in Chicago first, which I think my husband thought was going to be our final destination and figure out the next steps from there.

The time came for us to head out of Milton, and I was READY. As I was loading up the last of our things onto the truck, I shed a few tears looking at the emptiness of what I had come to know as home. I was close to so many people in that area and I knew I'd miss them dearly and to see me pack up our lives in such a way was overwhelming. I also understood and accepted that this was a door that God had closed and there was no turning back. We made the two-hour drive to Chicago with me driving our van and my husband driving the moving truck. When we arrived at my parents' house, I was a bit shocked but not a bit surprised when we lifted the door to the moving truck and found all our belongings destroyed. Everything was ruined to include my little aquarium I wanted to bring with us to Kentucky. Instead of being sad, I knew it was God allowing whatever happened to happen because his instruction was to leave EVERYTHING behind. I still told God yes in peace to leaving my past completely behind me and not even taking those things that represented what all we had come from into the new place he was leading us to.

We unloaded everything into the trash cans in the alley and nothing was salvageable by the time we emptied the whole truck. I asked my husband one more time if he was going to come to Kentucky with me and his adamant response again was "HECK NAW.."

My mother prepared a meal for us, and we all sat down together to eat. Afterwards, my husband made remarks about how he didn't care about what I was going to do but that he was going to take a nap so he could go out with his cousin when he woke up. I attempted to lay down with him but everything in me was unsettled and quite frankly aggravated with him because of how stubborn he was being about everything. He moved enough for us to leave where we were but refused to complete the instructions that God gave us. It was almost as if it was to spite both me and God to go as far as he had to make a point or prove that he was *not* going to do what I told him God instructed. I refused to move backwards into old thinking and settling for the familiar and comfortable. Chicago was a place that had always been comfortable for both of us, it was our hometown and it's exactly where we developed who we were everywhere else we had gone since leaving the first time. You know that saying, "everywhere you go, there you are?" I was not about to stay where I became the me that God was now calling me to rise above.

Some hours had gone by and as my husband laid there in a deep sleep, I heard a still voice say, "Go now." It made me nervous, but I obeyed immediately. I went and grabbed my children and got their things together and was ready to set on our way to Kentucky. My brother-in-law that had been staying with us all the while asked me if he was supposed to be getting his stuff together, but I had to tell him that he wasn't coming with us. It's not that I didn't want to take him, but I knew that would cause a different world of problems if I had taken him without my husband knowing. Bradley would have thrown a fit and that surely would've hindered what progress we were making to going, NOW. He began to cry, and I knew that it was time for us to leave quickly because he could easily have woken his brother up, and if he had, I would not leave at all.

I set him down with my parents in the kitchen, gave him a hug, packed the kids up in our van, and left. I had never really been a fan of making long drives by myself and I had a five hour trip ahead of me but something about it was so different than any other trip I'd taken. I felt consumed by a peace that not even I could understand but that I welcomed because it was confirmation that let me know that I was doing the right thing, that I was aligned with the Will of God, and that I was truly leaving my past behind me. It was still strange to think about the reality of starting over in a new and unfamiliar place, but it was worth it! The fears that tried to creep in were around the ideas of me having to leave my husband and my twelve-year-old brother-in-law and starting over.

The peace I had, however, was incomparable! To pull up to a new place, for a new beginning, already set up with electricity, water, and a phone was unreal! We didn't have furniture, but we had PEACE! When we got inside, my cell phone rang, and it was my husband. My heart dropped and reality truly set in, but I answered it anyway. He was MAD! He was yelling, asking where I was at and why I left his brother behind wherever I went but took the kids, and I told him flat out we left and were not coming back. I told him I didn't want to cross any lines taking his brother, so I had to leave him since we left the state. He didn't believe that we had left and that I'd taken our vehicle with us and that that was the reason I had left his brother. He said, "STOP PLAYING," as if he was having trouble processing what he really knew was true deep down.

To prove it to him, I gave him the number to the house and when he called it, I answered, I could hear in his moment of silence that it had sank in that we were gone. At first, he cussed me out I'm sure from the frustration of not being able to get to me and take that anger out on me and not having any control of the situation the way he was used to having. It felt nice knowing that the distance kept me from what could've been another abusive argument, but then I could hear his brother crying again, upset that I left him and now knowing that I didn't plan on coming back. He told him he didn't want to stay in Chicago with him and wanted to be with me wherever I was. We got off the phone and he called the next day with an entirely different tone. He said his brother had cried the whole day begging him to come with me and then he broke down crying on the phone! Almost in disbelief, I listened to him talk about how he missed me and the kids and how he didn't believe that I would leave him, especially not at my parent's house, to go on with the next chapter of our lives *without* him.

Another day had gone by, and he called again saying he didn't want to be without his family and that this has helped him to see what it really felt like for that to even be an option. I didn't know what else to say other than I was not coming back to Chicago and that if he truly felt that way, he would find a way to be with his family. To my surprise, he called me a few hours later telling me he had gotten a Greyhound ticket and would be on his way that night and arrive the following morning. I was not thrilled because here it is, the first time my husband decides he wants to stand for our marriage in a more positive light, it's to come and join me on a new journey that every part of me knew he'd bring his same old mindsets and ways along with him.

A big part of me was wishing he'd keep his word about never coming to Kentucky, but as sure as the day is long, I was there at the bus station to pick them up that next afternoon. When I saw them, his little brother was so excited to see me he ran and jumped into my arms. He hugged me tight and said, "please don't ever leave me again…" Part of me was hopeful to see that he'd pressed his way through to get to his family so quickly after we had left and saying he didn't want to be without us. I was without a doubt hesitant and doubtful on our lives being drastically different from what they were before I left, but there was still a piece of me that thought maybe this will be a new start in every way, for each of us and as he loaded the suitcases in the car, I was determined to be more optimistic about what life was going to be like from that point forward…

To be continued…

REFLECTION

When God is saying it's time to walk away, it's time to walk! The difficulty in that is usually our flesh opposing change and lack of familiarity and comfortability. Exodus means to come out, it means LIBERATION! God was pulling me into the next part of the journey and providing an escape from what was familiar and causing me to be stagnant in my growth as the woman He destined me to be and in my relationship with Him. God always provides the way, but the question is are we going to take it? Are we going to "go now" when He tells us to move? Are we going to leave everything when he says to leave EVERYTHING? When we find ourselves in circumstances we long to be liberated from, we must be able to discern God when He tells us the door is open and the opportunity is there, and we also have to be willing to tell him YES! So many times, we miss our exodus holding on tightly to those things or people we think we need or want in our lives, but God always has greater, we just have to trust that He knows more about our lives than we have planned for ourselves. Every experience, every place, and every relationship up to that point was a lesson I could never sit in a classroom to learn and none of those are lessons I'd wish to go back and repeat, but I'm grateful I endured the process up to moving away to Kentucky. God bought me out of my own version of Israel and was leading me to the promise land. Now the question is, on my new Journey of Hope, was I going to have an eleven-day trek through the wilderness that came next, or a forty-year journey?

CPSIA information can be obtained
at www.ICGtesting.com
Printed in the USA
BVHW052006160323
660607BV00006B/13